Spirit Guides for Beginners

The ultimate guide to spirit guides, contacting and communicating with your spirit guide, channelling the spirit world, and more!

Table Of Contents

Introduction 1

Chapter 1: Who And What Are Spirit Guides? 2

Chapter 2: How Do These Spirit Guides Help? 5

Chapter 3: Communicating With Your Spirit Guide 9

Chapter 4: Getting To Know Your Guides Better 12

Chapter 5: Differentiating Your Guide's Influence From Other Energies 16

Chapter 7: Spirit Guides in Religion 23

Chapter 8: Is It Safe to Contact Spirit Guides? 26

Chapter 9: How to Make Contact with Your Spirit Guide 33

Chapter 10: How You May Experience Your Spirit Guide 36

Chapter 11: What to Expect When Encountering a Spirit Guide 39

Chapter 12: Guardian Angels 42

Conclusion 44

Introduction

I want to thank you and congratulate you for picking up the book, "Spirit Guides for Beginners".

This is the recently updated 2nd edition, filled with new information making it the most up to date and complete guide to spirit guides for beginners available!

This book contains helpful information about spirit guides, what they are, and how you can make communication with yours.

The theory of spirit guides has existed for thousands of years in many different cultures. Although the names they give their guides may differ, there are many similarities.

Spirit guides are there to protect you from harm and negative entities, whilst guiding you on the right path. They are there to help you and to comfort you during the tough times.

This book will explain to you tips and techniques that will allow you to successfully understand and contact your spirit guides. Through making communication and establishing a relationship with you guides, you'll be able to better understand their suggestions for what choices you should make.

You will soon learn about the different spirit guides that most people have, what their purpose is, and how you can make communication with them!

Thanks again for taking the time to read this book, I hope you enjoy it!

Chapter 1:
Who And What Are Spirit Guides?

Spirit guides is a general term that's often used to describe an entity, in the form of a spirit that offers protection as well as guidance to a living human being. The idea of spirit guides is recognized by many different groups and individuals; spiritualist churches, psychics and mediums are among those who believe and even practice interaction with these guides. Certain ethnic groups also believe in the existence of spirit guides; just take the Native Americans, Egyptians and Chinese for example. Many of them attribute their ancient wisdom to these spirit guides and revere them as deities in most cases. Other popular associations when it comes to the term itself include: saints, enlightened leaders or masters, angels, nature spirits, guardian angels and totems. All of it depends upon the individual's personal belief.

One common denominator that many beliefs tend to share when it comes to the idea of spirit guides would be the fact that these entities are not always of human descent. Some of these spirit guides can exist in the form of energy or as light beings. There are those believed to have lived many different lives but have since paid their karmic debts; hence, they no longer have a need to reincarnate. There are groups that hold the belief that even animals can become spirit guides.

There is also the common belief that these spirit guides are actually assigned to every individual before they are even born. Their job is to provide us with the nudge that we need as well as enlightenment when it comes to choosing our path through life. They are responsible for aiding us in fulfilling certain spiritual "requirements", enabling us to gain better insight when it comes to our inner selves as well as the people around us. Some of these guides can stay with us through our entire life whilst there are those who leave once a particular phase is over, only to be replaced by another who will then walk us through the next chapter. Often these guides vary when it comes to their level of consciousness as well.

What do these spirit guides look like?

This is a question that a lot of people are curious about. It is hard to really tell what they look like because they don't always manifest with an actual human form. More often than not, what you'll be able to sense is either a feminine or a masculine energy. This is what they are, after all, energies that are around us. In some instances, however, these entities do take on certain forms. Some people have had the lovely opportunity of having a deceased relative as their spirit guide, though these cases can be quite rare. For younger children, it could be the spirit of a deceased pet or a family member they have never met but are connected to in some way.

How do these guides help us?

Spirit guides are ever-present and as such, they can see what is happening in our lives. However, they are not meant to always help out and will only intervene if the situation really calls for it. There are a number of different ways through which they can do this and paying attention will help you spot them early on. If you've ever heard of guardian angels, these spirit guides work in the same manner though they are not always the same entities.

Is it possible to get in touch with a spirit guide?

It is perfectly possible to get in touch and even befriend your spirit guide. However, it isn't just a matter of simply speaking to them out of the blue and expecting a reply. Keep in mind that they exist in a different plane altogether and for us to be able to interact with them, we need to develop our spirituality more. The process can take time and plenty of practice as well as knowledge on how to do it; if you're willing and your guide is too, then communication is certainly possible.

Are there good and bad spirit guides?

The answer would be: YES. However, one cannot consider a bad entity as a spirit guide as their purpose for being with you is very different. Because they do exist, it is important for a person to be conscious about their spirit guide as well as the influence it has on them. Just because they seem to be helping you, it doesn't necessarily mean that their intentions are good as well. Mediums and psychics would know this well and often advise people to listen to their intuition with regards to spirit guides. If something feels off, then look into it and remember to be cautious.

How many spirit guides can a person have?

The number of spirit guides any person could have varies a lot. Typically, it would be around four to seven guides, but this can change a lot depending on the person. This is, of course, not counting the angelic presence that may be around as well. A person would have one primary guide, a few others which are temporary and some that are meant to be with you only for certain situations; these are called special assignment guides. The defining factor for the amount of guides that a person has would be their current situation in life. If someone needs more guidance when compared to another person, you can be sure that they will have a few extra guides to help get them through the struggles they have.

Chapter 2:
How Do These Spirit Guides Help?

There are many different ways through which your guide can help you. Some of them are meant to walk you through your childhood and teenage years. There are those that will come to you once you've reached early adulthood. Their assistance can vary in nature but whether it be something practical or spiritual, one cannot deny that it really is something special once you're able to recognize the signs. To do this, you must understand what your guide's purpose is and how they can help you.

It has been said that their role is to provide us with consistent nudges, almost always done intuitively, in order to keep us moving forward and on the right track. If there is a certain goal that we must accomplish, they will lead us onto the right path and even carefully place people in our way who might be able to help. Resources, books - even help with our finances; anything that will get us to where we need to be, basically. Should we feel lost along the way, they can also provide us with both comfort and insight. Of course, this isn't something that we're always able to see. In fact, very few people are able to recognize the work of a spirit guide.

But how do they intervene exactly? We've already established the fact that they are capable of seeing everything that happens to us but how do they influence our actions without being obvious? Here are some of the ways:

- By sending signs. Your guides are capable of putting together certain things to get you to pay attention or provide you with important hints. You may see these are no more than coincidences but pay attention because more often than not, they are supposed to mean something for you. Try and be more aware of what goes on around you. You wouldn't want to miss out on something good.

- Gut feelings. Have you ever had that sinking feeling in your stomach but you can't quite place where it came from? That's quite literally what a gut feeling is. It's easy to mistake it for a nervous tic but if you pay closer attention, it can also mean something else. It can be that feeling you get when someone is being false; that unshakeable notion that something is off about them but you can't quite put a finger on it. That could just be your guide giving your gut a gentle poke and cautioning you from trusting that particular person.

- Messages through your intuition. The thing with most people is that they tend to tune out their intuition, preferring the facts that they can see and calculate physically. While this is understandable, being in touch with this side of you can also provide you with a wealth of valuable information. Your guides can send you flashes of insight, such as that sudden voice inside your head warning you of an incoming car while you're crossing the street. It could also be that voice that warns you in whispers about a cheating lover or husband. Try and learn how to listen to your intuition more; give it more trust as well for it can certainly aid you in many of your endeavors.

- Sending certain people into your life. There are those among us who believe that there are no such things as coincidences. If this is the case then it only means that people come into our lives for a reason. When you put guides into the picture, this makes more sense. Some guides can end up putting their "charges" together, a kind of chance meeting that is meant to influence their lives in one way or another. Have you ever found yourself thinking about someone from the past constantly and then unexpectedly seeing them again some days after? How about that time when you were craving a bit of change in your life and within a few days, you meet someone who could offer you exactly that? While it feels like serendipity, consider that it might have actually been a set up.

- Nudges and subtle influences on a daily basis. As humans, we are quite prone to making the wrong decisions even with the help of our spirit guides. Should this happen, they can actually arrange for certain things to happen. These are small nudges that would put us back on the right track. For example, you could be running late to a meeting but your car keys go missing inexplicably. You know you placed them in your bag before you went to bed so it's impossible, right? Then the phone begins to ring and it turns out to be quite the life-changing phone call. After a while, you find your keys in the most obvious place. If you had found them earlier, however, you would have missed that important phone call. Now, things get tricky for spirit guides because people have free will. You could have just opted to get a cab and left the house anyway, missing the phone call. They can only influence us to some extent so the better we are at taking cues from their hints, the better.

Now, while all of that sounds great, what you must know is that your spirit guides cannot help you all the time. This is because your guides will only help you accomplish the goals that you have set for yourself long before you even incarnated. If it isn't your soul's purpose, then your spirit guides cannot help you with it, no matter how much you ask or will them to.

Chapter 3:
Communicating With Your Spirit Guide

One way of understanding the signs they give us would be to get to know the guides better. While you don't need highly developed psychic abilities to do this, it will require some practice and connection with your intuition (sixth sense) in order for it to be successful. Do remember that whilst you're not able to interact with them just yet, they are able to fully perceive you. All you really need to do is address them in the right way.

But how does one do that? Do we have to speak out loud or speak to them through the mind? You can communicate with them using both ways. Whenever you think of a particular thought, this instantly creates energy - one that can be perceived by your guides. Casting a thought out, one that's focused on a certain energy, will be received. For example, if you want some help when it comes to finding love or success, all you need to do is meditate on that thought and focus your energy on it. Your spirit guide is listening.

- Meditation. There are countless things that could distract you from focusing on what it is that you need. The noise of the people you live with, worries with regards to your work and so on. Meditating will help quiet all of these things down, allowing you to concentrate your energy as well as open your chakras. The more sensitive you are to a higher plane, the better you will be at communicating with the spirit guides.

- Talking to them in the same way you would talk to any of your friends. This might seem odd if you were to do it in a more public place as you'll appear to be speaking to yourself, so do it at home where it's nice and quiet. The first few times, you may feel as if it isn't working or that you're not getting any response. This is fine, it will take you some practice in order to become more in tune and increase your awareness of the subtle things they do. Keep on communicating a few times each day. This will help you practice and strengthen your connection with them.

Now, you might be wondering, why is this needed? If your guide is able to perceive everything about you, then they should be able to know when and how they could be of assistance, right? However, this is not always the case. Most of the time, they are bound to not doing anything especially if their actions would violate your individual free will. As such, a conscious request for their help is needed. Whenever you do, some of your vital life force is transferred to them and this will aid them in accomplishing your request. From the spiritual realm, they will manifest something into the physical. It really is an amazing thing once you're able to see how it all works.

Things to Remember:

- Ask politely but do not pray to your spirit guides. Those who were raised with a religious background have been taught that in order to gain the help of something spiritual, one must pray or in some cases, beg for their favor. However, this is not the case with your guides. They are able to view the world from a different perspective and see the bigger picture, but they answer to something higher than them, much like you. Remember that they are not your superiors.

- Asking repeatedly will not make your request happen much quicker. This is especially so if what you're asking for is something that is not meant for you; something that is not in your purpose to have. Winning the lottery? If it is of no use to you in the grand scheme of things, you can trust that it won't be given. We've already established that the spirit guides know what is needed and what you have to achieve, they work according to this pattern and they will not deviate. So even if you ask repeatedly or even beg, this might amuse them but do very little to convince them of doing those things for you.

Remember to be grateful and show gratitude. Actions such as these are often returned in kind and it will also help you develop a better relationship with your guide. After all, though their actions are subtle and their presence is not always felt, they are working tirelessly to help you achieve your purpose. Offer them your thanks as you would a friend who has helped you through tough times. There's no need for rituals or grand actions, simply thanking them and recognizing what they do is often more than enough.

Chapter 4:
Getting To Know Your Guides Better

Your guides have names and a certain role in the team they're in. If you're lucky, you might even get to know what they look like. All of these things are important knowledge if you really want to form a bond with your guide. After all, would you start a friendship with someone without knowing who they are? Initiate this with your guide once you have learned how to communicate with them.

Certain guides will have names or in some cases, make use of pseudonyms. You can find out what this is through communication but if you're unable to properly decipher the responses that you're being given, then contacting someone who would be able to will help. Remember that you have more than one guide and getting to know each one of them will certainly be an enlightening experience. Beyond their name and their role, a medium would be able to inform you of all the ways these guides have helped you. With that, you'll be able to form a clearer picture of how they have guided you to where you are now.

Another way of getting to know your guides would be through understanding their preferred way of influencing or interacting with you. Whenever they communicate, your guides will choose a medium for their messages, one that they know you're quite adept at using. Every person possesses a certain intuitive gift, some may have developed it more than others but these gifts are certainly there. Clairaudience, clairvoyance, claircognizance and clairsentience cover all of the possible ways through which a spirit guide may contact you.

If you're the kind of person who's more visual than anything else, your spirit guide might choose to appear in your mind's eye with their message, or provide you with an image that you associate with something meaningful. If you happen to be claraudient, you might begin to notice an inner voice that whispers guidance or inspiration to you. Their messages could also come in the form of song lyrics which appear in your head out of the blue. For those who are claircognizant, their guides may "download" the messages or information to them, usually in the form of thoughts. As for those who are clairsentient, they will physically feel these things. A tickling sensation in the back of their ear or a shiver where there ought to be none. Try becoming more aware of the different sensations that happen to you, this would help you get better at recognizing which ones are from your spirit guides.

Different Types Of Guides:

- Protectors. These guides tend to be strong in both manner and character. Their physical attributes tend to match this as well, appearing like warriors or soldiers. Depending on where you live, protector guides tend to be of indigenous heritage to that place. For example, in North America, many people have Native American protector guides but there are also those who look like Vikings in terms of appearance. Some protector guides are also not human. Larger animals such as lions, panthers and elephants can also become protectors and be called upon whenever you're in need. Strength, bravery, security - these are some of the things that your protectors can aid you with.

- Door and Gate Keepers. These guides are a bit like your protectors but unlike them, the keepers work in order to keep the negative (also known as lower vibrational) energies away from the person. This is especially so if that particular person is trying to open doorways to other realms; the keepers would only allow the appropriate spirits to pass through. They are the guides that offer both psychic and physical protection for mediums as well as spirit communicators. If you're really looking to increase your access to the spiritual realm, you would want to get to know your gatekeepers better and create a stronger connection with them.

- Messengers. Also known as message bearers, these guides assist us when it comes to developing our own ability to accept and send messages into the spirit world. They are also capable of both finding as well as obtaining certain information that we may need. If you're clairaudient, it would be beneficial to work with the messengers as they will be able to help you hone your abilities. Mediums and psychics always ask for the aid of these guides during readings as they might require information that only they can procure.

- Healers. Healing guides (also known as Doctor guides) are the ones that help us when it comes to our health and overall well-being. Any person who works in the field of healing, whether it be through energy or actual surgeries, tend to have very strong healing guides. Some may even say that these guides help in steadying their hands and keeping the minds focused whenever they're working. We all connect with our healing guides in one way or another and they are also the ones that nudge us towards the direction of living healthier should they see us straying. The guides themselves may have been healers during their time on earth. Monks, energy healers and shamans appear quite a lot.

- Teachers. These guides are natural educators and their role is to aid us when it comes to finding spiritual growth. They may point us to certain books that we need to read or even seek out classes for us which would be able to help further our improvement. These guides might also connect us with people whose roles would be to teach us and bring us new experiences from which we can learn. The teachers help us in better understanding both the spiritual and philosophical aspects of any study we undertake in our lifetime. If you've been feeling like you lack something in the spiritual side of your life, call on the teachers for some guidance. They just might know the right people to place along your path.

- Joy or Happiness Guides. These particular guides are meant to bring more joy and laughter into our lives. They are the ones that remind us to enjoy life a bit more, to loosen up a bit more when we become too serious. They typically take the form of small children or even entities that are often associated with merriment. If you've been going through a rough patch and can't seem to see the silver lining in your daily life, call upon your Joy guide and let them bring you what you need in order to feel peace as well as light-heartedness once more.

Other guides that you must also be aware of include: Short-term guides, chemistry and energy guides, totem and power animal guides, deva and earth spirit guides as well as those that watch over entire families. It is important for people to know their guide's purpose as this will allow them to better know who to consult or ask should they require something in particular.

Chapter 5:
Differentiating Your Guide's Influence From Other Energies

Our guides always have our best interests at heart but the fact is, they are not the only energies that surround us. Remember the ones that they protect us from? Those entities can also influence us in negative ways. This is why it is also important for us to learn how to differentiate the input that our guides give us and the input that comes from somewhere else. This can be a little tricky but here are a few things to remember which might help you better distinguish which is which.

- The influence that you receive from your guides will always feel uplifting and is able to raise your consciousness just a bit more. It will respect your free will and honor the fact that you are the only conscious creator of your life and as such, you are responsible for it. The only thing they can do is provide nudges and some aid - but only if you ask for it. In comparison, a negative entity that's trying to influence you would be pushy and aggressive. They can even encourage you to completely abdicate responsibility.

- Remember that guides will not tell you what to do but instead, provide you with suggestions. They can also drop hints about a particular course of action that works well with the path that you should take but in the end, they would leave everything up to you. Keep in mind that they respect your free will as a person and would never push anything that you don't want to do or could endanger you.

- Your guides will never get angry with you or threaten you with anything. They will never berate you or make you feel bad about yourself. Instead, they are very patient and are also capable of providing you with the comforting you might need at any given moment. However, while they might think you're great, it is not in their character to flatter you until your ego bloats. They will not encourage you to put yourself above others. This is because they understand that doing these things will not help you and will not serve their agenda as well.

- Spirit guides know and have faith in your capacity to get through the rough patches and issues you may have in your life. There will be bad days, after all. They will be there for you, yes, and show an immense amount of compassion but never will they throw you a pity party. Instead, they would try to motivate you and get you moving forward so that you can get on with doing something more productive. On the other hand, a negative entity that's trying to influence you might actually indulge your self-pity and make you feel even worse. They feed upon this and the more vulnerable you get, the easier it is for them to manipulate you.

There are also certain warning signs that you should be aware of. Remember, not every influence around you is good and that applies to different entities that might try and coax you into doing something as well. Here are a few precautions:

- Your guide constantly communicates with you about secret portals or doorways that they have managed to open. They might brag about the fact that they were the only ones to ever do it. An actual spirit guide will not deal with trivial matters because it doesn't serve their purpose.

- Strange things have begun happening ever since you've established contact with your spirit guide. Though your guide claims to be protecting you from all these things, you may also notice a pattern in the weird occurrences and their appearances. Pay more attention.

- The spirit is coaxing you to do certain rituals which would supposedly help improve your situation or get you what you need. No proper spirit guide would have you do this just to fulfill your request. If the request serves your purpose, they wouldn't question or demand anything and just do it for you.

- Your spirit guide is asking you to become an instrument for something that they want to do and in exchange, they will do one of your bigger requests. They might tempt you with something that you've been really wanting or have been asking for repeatedly. Again, your spirit guide would not demand anything of you so do avoid any entity that may ask you to do this.

- They whisper negative words in your ear. As we have already established, these spirit guides are meant to uplift and enlighten your soul. They are not supposed to break you down even further with words. So do beware of this kind of influence and avoid it.

Why are the guides helping you? What is their personal agenda?

Your spirit guides are not at all different from us. Besides the fact that they don't have a corporeal body, they are still quite human much like all of us. They know what it's like to have a body and to live in our reality. However, they have managed to evolve beyond that point of requiring to reincarnate and as such, they are pursuing their soul's next phase: being a spirit guide. In assisting you, they are also helping themselves towards the path of evolution. This is a win-win situation for you and them. However, whilst it might seem that they're not doing you that big of a favor, gratitude is something that they do appreciate receiving and as such, be sure to always thank yours.

Can your guide spirit be someone you knew from this life?

Yes, there is a chance that you know or may have been associated with your spirit guide in this lifetime. There are some who believe that their guide is someone who loved them dearly such as a grandparent, a parent, a sibling or even a pet. Whilst this could happen, it is most likely that your guide is someone not related to you. However, keeping in mind that we made agreements with these spirits before we were ever born into this world, we can safely say that we do know them but the memory just isn't there.

Also, because someone close to you has recently passed away doesn't necessarily mean that they'll become one of your guides. Whilst their souls might stay with you and even provide you with guidance should you need it, they do not become an "official" guide. On the subject of deceased pets becoming spirit guides, the same applies. It is not uncommon for pets to linger around and help you through the whole grieving process but at some point, once they feel like you no longer need them, they do move on. Animal totems are different, of course.

Chapter 6: Types of Spirit Guides

The descriptions of spirit guides tend to differ depending on what particular faith or belief you follow, but one thing connects everything: Spirit guides are meant to help us through life. Think enlightenment during confusing periods and nudges towards the right direction whenever we're veering off of our life path.

Though previously mentioned, below is a more in-depth look at the different types of guides you may encounter.

Different Types of Guides:

Protectors

These guides are quite strong in both manner and character. If they have corporeal forms, they are often large and strong in appearance. Most of the time, your protector guide would be of indigenous heritage and related to your own ancestry. For example, people in North America would often have Native American protector guides whilst some might have ones that appear quite similar to Vikings. Most of the time, they are human, though there are instances wherein animals take the role of protector guides. Panthers, elephants and wolves are quite common as they represent strength and courage well. These are the guides that you can call upon whenever you are in need of a little bravery. Think of them as guardian angels as they serve the same purpose.

Door and Gatekeeper Guides

These guides are quite similar to the protectors in that they help drive away any lower vibe (negative) energies away from you, making sure that they don't drain any of your own energy.

This is especially useful if you regularly practice opening doorways to different realms as you would need to make sure that only the right spirits are allowed entry. These guides are also capable of providing you with psychic as well as physical protection—something that both mediums and spirit communicators would greatly benefit from. If you are more "open" to spirits and other energies, the presence of Door and Gatekeeper guides will also help keep you safe. Connect with your Gatekeeper guide whenever you're attempting to open up to the spiritual realm or initiating spiritual communication.

Message Bearer

These types of guides help improve our own ability to hear, get and deliver messages coming from the spirit world. Message bearer guides also help us when it comes to obtaining and finding certain information that we might need, regardless of the purpose we have for it. These guides are most beneficial to people who are clairaudient and are seeking to develop their abilities further in order to help others. The same applies to mediums and psychics, as well as anyone who work with akashic records, as message bearer guides are capable of providing them with the information they need.

These guides will often appear in the form of a bird to their wards; and because of their ability to travel great distances in a short amount of time, they are also able to obtain the information needed very quickly.

Healers

Healer guides, also known as doctor guides, help us when it comes to our overall health and well-being. People, who work in a healing or medical profession, whether it be traditional or modern, would certainly have a strong healing guide around them. More often than not, these guides used to be healers themselves whilst they were still living. From monks, shamans and energy healers, they were the ones who managed to maintain their knowledge and skills, passing it on to whoever they find deserves and needs it most. Call upon them whenever you're feeling weary or under the weather.

Professor or Teachers

As the name suggests, these guides are educators and are the ones who help guide us through the path towards our spiritual growth. They will often direct you to certain things you might need at the moment: books that you ought to read, classes that you should take and even introduce you to people who will help further you along. These guides assist us when it comes to gaining an understanding of the spiritual as well as the philosophical aspects of the studies we undertake in our lifetime. Call upon them if you are looking to discover more about yourself spiritually and they will help put things together in order to make it happen for you.

Joy/Happiness Guides

These are the guides whose purpose is to bring laughter and joy into our lives. They are the ones who remind us to lighten up and to find pleasure in the simple things. More often than not, these guides come in the form of small children or fairies providing us with lighthearted energy and helping tide us through the more difficult times. Call upon them whenever you feel broken down and weary. They can bring a smile to your face and help you see the positive side in any situation you might find yourself in.

Chapter 7:
Spirit Guides in Religion

Spirit guides tend to very according to one's religion or beliefs. They take on many different forms and are referred to using a number of differing names, but there are always be underlying similarities between each one. Just take the protector guides for example, they are referred to as guardian angels in certain beliefs.

Here are some of the most common types of spirit guides which can be found in different religions:

The Ascended Masters or Enlightened Ones

These categories of guides are often made up of the spirits that have led a very spiritual life during their time on earth. In death, they moved onto a higher spiritual plane, otherwise known as enlightenment. The best examples for this would be spiritual guides such as Krishna, Jesus and Buddha. The Ascended masters would typically work with a collective group of souls, though their primary focus is to help all of humanity. For people who regularly work with energy using different techniques such as Reiki, they always tap into the wisdom provided by these masters.

Ancestral Guides

Ancestral guides are the ones who have some form of kinship with you. When it comes to closeness, this would vary and there's no real explanation as to how or why certain people are assigned to you. Your guide could come in the form of your favorite aunt to even a long-dead ancestor that you never even knew of. In certain religions/beliefs, these spirits are often seen as reincarnated guides—the souls of those who have loved us during their lifetime or someone who has some form of blood connection to you through family. They appear in many different religions and faiths as teachers and guiding spirits who have your utmost well-being in mind. More often than not, these guides stay with their ward for a certain length of time—some believe them to stick around through an entire lifetime in order to make sure that the person they're watching over doesn't stray from their path.

Common Spirit Guides

Common spirit guides can by symbolic, archetypical or symbolic of something that might mean a lot to you and your journey. They appear in many different religions and beliefs—also typically known as angels. These guides don't often stay throughout your life and will only be present during significant moments, often delivering a change in direction when it comes to your path. It is during this time that they would nudge you towards where you need to go. They might introduce you to people who will help guide you along or speak to you through various means, providing you with information and letting you know what needs to be done. Once their job is done, however, these guides will move on. You might meet them along the way once more, but it is rare that they end up staying longer than they ought to.

Animal Guides

These types of guides are more commonly associated with Native American or Shamanic beliefs. However, there are people who do claim to have animal spirit guides that come in the form of deceased pets. These particular entities are considered to be more of a companion type guide instead of one that provides wisdom and information needed for spiritual growth. That being said, there are faiths that believe in people having animal totems which are capable of acting as a protector and a teacher.

Chapter 8:
Is It Safe to Contact Spirit Guides?

Whenever you open yourself to Spirit Guide communication, you must understand that you are also opening yourself to the spirit world. Some people are more open when it comes to others, but for the most part, the precautions that one must take are the same. Is it safe to contact your guides? The answer is: YES. However, you must make sure that you do things properly. Consider the fact that there are other energies around you at this very moment and not all of those are positive or would treat you in the same regard as your guide would.

Knowledge is important. The more aware you are, the better and safer it is for you. This doesn't mean that you should devote a lot of time studying. Some people do undertake this field of study, but having enough knowledge of the basics should be enough when you're first starting out. Another thing you have to remember is to never play with an Ouija board. There is no way of filtering the entities that might get through to you and in case you were not aware, negative spirits can easily pretend to be your Spirit Guide in order to gain your trust. There are few things that might be able to help you tell the difference, but this only applies if you've known your guide for a certain length of time.

Now that we have that out of the way, here are few tips to help you get started with contacting your guides safely:

Start with a Prayer

Whenever you are attempting to create a connection with your Spirit Guide, always start with a prayer and request for the presence of only the spirits who have the best intentions for you at heart. A simple prayer such as, "I wish to make contact with my Spirit Guide and for them to approach and make contact with me. Only the highest vibration of spirits is allowed to make communication, the spirits who come from the pure light of the Holy Spirit, amen." Be specific when it comes to this and make sure that you are sincere in your prayer in order for it to be heard.

We Attract Spirits When We Think About Them

If you should sense a spirit around whilst you're in meditation, you can request for them manifest or ask them for any messages that they have to deliver and just feel the power of their presence. Whenever you ask them a question, make sure that you stay in an open state, allowing answers to come through. If there are no images being sent, just feel their presence and find enjoyment in this manifestation. Feeling their presence can also help strengthen the connection you have with them.

If you happen to see a spirit through your mind's eye, communicate using all of your senses. Feel their presence and allow this vision to form. Listen to check if they are trying to tell you anything. Spirits tend to be attracted to the person who thinks of them because they see this as that person's way of calling for them. They hear this call in the spiritual realm and then come to you. This is also the reason why it is quite common for people to feel the presence of their loved ones whenever they are thought of.

Spirit Guides Will Not Appear To You With Any Physical Disabilities

If you happen to encounter a spirit who has deformities or if you receive energy that is angry, unhappy or confused then this might be an earth bound spirit, or what's known as a ghost, and not a spirit guide. In the beginning of your practice, it would be wise to avoid contact with such spirits. If you encounter any spirit who makes you feel uncomfortable, just say the prayer for protection again until you feel their presence disappear and you start feeling comfortable again.

Another thing you can do is visualize a shield of white light surrounding you which allows only the highest vibration spirits to enter. You can also ask for your Angels to come in and take away any of the low vibration spirits in your surroundings. Once your spirit guides manifest, these uncomfortable spirits should be gone. After you have advanced with your experiences and knowledge, you can choose to deal with these earth bound spirits and help them through the process of crossing over. It isn't always easy and the work itself might be tedious, but if you find purpose in doing so then by all means do it.

Keep a Journal of Your Experiences

For beginners, and even for more advanced practitioners, it is always a good idea to keep a journal of your experiences after communicating with your guides. Often, you might find that a message gradually becomes clearer when you start writing it down. When you're in that moment of receiving information you are in a state of no resistance. When this happens, you are actually using more of the right side of brain, and writing things down allows you to switch into a different mode of remembering and analyzing. This transition from right brain to left brain can actually help you with recalling things better, and understanding any of the little details you may have missed otherwise.

Write as if you're going to send this journal to someone else. Try and explain your experiences in as much detail as possible so that when you do read it later, you will be able to visualize the entire experience in a more vivid way. In some cases, you may receive more information as you write; this is called the "automatic writing session". This enables you to switch from using your right brain to left brain easily since you are still tapping into the spirit realm and are not too focused on what your own belief system is trying to tell you. Plenty of significant and insightful information can come through in this manner.

Don't Do Anything Out Of The Norm For You

Keep in mind that these spirits would not typically give out orders and tell you what you "have" to do. They will not tell you that you need to separate from your husband/wife or risk your money in any form of investment. Nothing of that sort. The job of a spirit guide is to show you which of the many paths is best to take as well as why this is so. You are supposed to take the information you're provided then give it some consideration, weighing it along with all the other knowledge you have before making a final decision.

The role of your spirit guide is to provide you with insight on all things physical as well as spiritual before nudging you towards a decision. They are here to provide you with spiritual guidance and it is not their job to be a dictator. See it as more of a joint project between you and them. On the other hand, you have low vibration spirits who will often try their hardest to influence you into making decisions which are not always of the positive kind. Keep in mind that these types of spirits would often harbor bad intentions. If you're just starting out, you might experience some difficulty when trying to distinguishing your Spirit Guide from other spirits. Trust your instinct. If the information feels good to you then it is safe to say that it comes from your spirit guide. If it doesn't then don't risk anything without considering things twice over.

Experiencing Physical Sensations Is Normal

It's the same kind of sensations that you feel whenever you're meditating. You might feel these sensations around your head, neck, ears, back as well as other parts of your body. This could be an indication that your Spirit Guides are working with healing energy or working on your electromagnetic system as a means of helping you become more sensitive to receiving spirit communications. The most interesting thing about this is that these sensations usually come after or in between working on your spirit communication and development, as opposed to during. The most common sensations can include things like:

- *Tingling Sensation*

- *Prickly Sensation*

- *Feeling Hot/Cold*

- *Hot Spots*

Meditation

Meditation is the practice of sitting quietly, while regulating your breathing using mantras or visualization. This is all done in an attempt to harmonize your mind, body and soul. Why is it important for Spirit communication? Well, because meditation is effective when it comes to clearing the mind of any clutter it may contain. Think of it as knocking out two birds with one stone as it works on both the spiritual and physical levels.

Think about it this way: You clean your house, take showers to keep yourself clean, eat the right kind of food and maintain your physical health by making sure you get proper rest. It is equally important to your physical and spiritual health to keep your mind as well as your energetic field free of clutter, as doing so allows you to operate at your most efficient level.

Be Patient!

A lot of people do struggle with being patient when it comes to spirit communication. It is a matter of constant practice and development—you will not be able to successfully do this overnight and even if you manage to, there would be risks to it. Some people take years in order to properly communicate with their spirit guides and receive the information they need easily. Development is a constant aspect of this and you will have to continuously learn, as well as improve in order to better your connection with your guide. No, you do not have to make a living out of it and it need not take up a lot of your time. An hour a day of practice when done consistently can produce a significant difference when it comes to your abilities.

Be patient and remember to stay committed to what you're doing. This is a test of sincerity for some people as well. There are those who only learn it as a means of making money or even bragging to others that they have the particular skill. Without the passion for it, a person can easily lose patience and grow frustrated over the slow process. Not only will you need to be disciplined with yourself, you also have to know that this is something you really want. Don't turn it into a hobby simply because you're interested at the moment. Once you connect and communicate with your spirit guide, it is something that you need to maintain. There are plenty of benefits, of course, but building that connection is the most important aspect of the process.

Chapter 9:
How to Make Contact with Your Spirit Guide

When it comes to contacting your spirit guide, having the ability to clear your mind is definitely a must. It is considered by many to be a fundamental tool that will help you to achieve spiritual development. Now, there is a simple way to contact your spirit guide. Follow it step by step and with enough practice, you should be able to communicate with your guide freely, and safely.

Shall we get started?

- Begin by placing yourself in a quiet state of mind. Sit on a chair and close your eyes, quietly asking your guide to move closer to you and let their presence be known. Do understand that this isn't an instant thing, so don't worry if you can't feel any sensations at first.

- Patience is key. Give it time and don't expect them to manifest as soon as you ask them to. They might give certain signals, however, so keep yourself open to these things. You might see images in your mind's eye or they might draw your attention towards something. Pay attention.

- If you start feeling the energy around you change, this might indicate that they are coming forward. Trust what you're getting and never rush the process. Just let things happen.

- Next, ask the presence to provide you a sign so you'll known when they are around you. This can come in the form of a fragrance, a sound, or anything that you are able to easily recognize. It depends upon how well you communicate with your guide. If you're communicating with more than one, different scents can allow you to differentiate one from the other.

- In some cases, you can ask these guides for a name you can use to refer to them. You won't always get an answer straight away, this is normal. It may take a few days, even some months before you get any reply from their part. The name itself will often enter your subconscious without much effort. It can appear whilst you're meditating or even while you're doing everyday tasks. When it does, just go with it.

- As the communication and connection between you and your guides strengthens, you can also begin to ask them to manifest in the form of physical sensations. They can create goosebumps or touch your face whenever they're around. It isn't uncommon for people to feel their guide's physical presence after months of communication. Ask them to hold your hand and see if you feel anything after. Their presence will always have an effect on us so just wait and trust what you get.

The Four Fundamentals for Living Successfully while working with Spirit Guides:

- Ask: Whenever asking, always be specific. This is because they won't be able to help you unless you personally ask them. Keep in mind that these guides are not allowed to help you unless you request for it. They cannot intrude upon your free will or do things without your bidding. Do not be afraid to ask for spiritual as well as material gifts. Simple things such as parking spots or for motivation during work—all these things are in their capacity to provide for you. Believe and you shall receive!

- Believe: After you have made your request, believing that it will manifest is also important. Trust that your guide will provide you with your request if they think it would help you along your path.

- Let it Happen: This particular step requires quite a bit of patience. It's all about letting go and allowing your spirit guides to fulfill their work. Do your best to not meddle—in fact, meddling only shows them that you do not trust in them fully. Don't repeat your wishes too much; they heard you the first time. The response will never be instantaneous. Give it some time, continue with the work you need to do and let things unfold in their own time.

- Thank You: Remember to give thanks when you do get what you ask for. Even when it doesn't happen as you hoped it would, give thanks to your guides for leading you towards the right path. The thing is, there may be instances wherein you won't get exactly what you asked for. Instead, you will be provided with what you need, the thing that will bring you to your highest good.

Chapter 10:
How You May Experience Your Spirit Guide

There are many different ways through which our Spirit Guides communicate. It can vary from one person to the other and there are times when, once ample connection has been established, you can create your own "exclusive" means of communication; something that you'll be able to easily recognize without much shadow of doubt.

For beginners, however, knowing the basics should be enough. These guides do have go-to methods when it comes to communicating and all you need to do is open yourself a bit more to it. To help you understand better, here are a few examples.

- **Listen to your intuition.** The little voice in your head that tells you to slow down whenever you're driving too fast or to simply notice something that you otherwise wouldn't have—these are often communications from your guides or even from your higher self. Most people tend to disregard these things, but if you try to listen, you might get positive results from it. Some people have even noticed recurring patterns that they would normally ignore. It may not be easy to separate your ego from your guide at first, but with constant awareness you should become more familiar with differentiating one from the other.

- **Go with your gut.** Ever heard of the saying: "Follow your gut"? Well, it is something that you might want to take to heart. Your guides might be using this to direct you towards a certain path that you ought to be following. For example, if you're discussing business with people you've only recently met, but your gut is telling you that they are reliable then you might want to listen. That good feeling whenever you meet people for the first time? Take that into consideration as well. Other than the fact that energy often speaks louder than words, your guides might also be nudging you towards developing a connection with these people as they know they would help you achieve your goals. The same applies if you are getting negative vibes from certain people. If this happens, be wary of them.

- **Watch for signs.** These can both be the easiest and hardest to spot. Always ask your guides for what you need and check for any signs that would indicate if you've been heard or not. You can even ask for specific signs, though they may always choose a different method. For example, some people ask their guides to show them something interesting in order to confirm that they've been heard. If after this request, you find certain things to be recurring—do consider this as something out of the ordinary. Sometimes, your guides might send you messages through these signs even without you requesting for anything. If your guide wants you to read a particular book, they might make sure that you always stumble upon it. The repeated encounter might help you see that this particular book would be of some use to you. It's easy to dismiss these things as no more than mere coincidences, but pay attention. There might be more to it than that and it's always worth listening to your spirit guide.

Your spirit guides will communicate using various methods. It might also depend upon your ability to perceive the messages they have to deliver. The methods may not always be obvious, but these subtle nudges are something you should try and pay more attention to. Patterns will emerge once you do, and who knows? If you've been seeking change or answers to questions you've been harboring, then becoming more aware of these messages might provide you with exactly what you need. So go on, listen to what your spirit guides have to say.

Chapter 11:
What to Expect When Encountering a Spirit Guide

1. Whilst your guides are capable of getting you to where you need to be, making sure that your path aligns with your soul's purpose, it is not their job to decide what you should do with your life. A lot of people tend to think that their spirit guide will provide them with exactly this: A PURPOSE. However, this is not the case. It is completely up to you to decide what you want to do. You are responsible for the intentions you set and your guides are only there to provide you with the proper guidance to help you achieve your goals. Don't expect them to do everything for you.

    When you're setting your intentions, try to be firm and specific with them. Your guides can end up getting mixed signals and become confused as to what it is you really need if you fail to do this. As said earlier, your guides are not capable of reading your mind. You cannot expect them to help out if you're completely undecided about what it is that you actually want. Try not to waste their guidance and give yourself some time to formulate your intentions—don't rush.

    Expect your guide to provide you with information about important decisions that you're going to make, but do know that everything is up to you in the end. You can choose to take their advice or opt for what you have personally decided on. Since they cannot influence your thoughts and actions, you need not worry about them having a negative on your choices. With that said, it is always wise to consider the messages that they give you.

2. Now, when we talk about messages and insight—remember that these get delivered in a subtle manner. At times, if one is not observant enough or not sensitive to the communications of their spirit guide, these messages are easily missed. This is one thing you ought to expect from your guides and is also something that you must learn how to tap into.

   This might be confusing, especially for beginners, as it can be difficult to differentiate your intuition from actual messages from your guide. However, this becomes easier the more you develop your connection with them. You'll become more familiar with their way of communicating with you.

   Another thing to keep in mind when it comes to your guides is that their messages won't come every hour. Typically, they'll send you no more than one a day in order to avoid overwhelming you. Just imagine getting non-stop messages from them and how confusing, and dizzying that could be.

3. Your guides will never force you to do anything that they know you aren't capable of or is completely outside of your norm. Whilst they are referred to as guides, you cannot expect them to provide you with blunt directions as to what you need to do. However, do expect them to let you know when you're straying from the right path. This is another aspect to the messages they send you. Aside from insight, they are also meant to nudge you towards the things you should be doing. As discussed earlier, they can do this through different ways. All you really need to be is intuitive towards these "nudges".

Are the guides ever wrong? Rarely. Consider that the information you're being provided comes from an enlightened source, a divine source of wisdom that you're able to tap into through your guides. The application of the information is another matter, of course. How you interpret the signs and messages can greatly influence the outcome. Yes, you might make mistakes in translating them and some details might get lost during this process—don't fret! This is normal and you'll eventually get better with continuous practice.

Chapter 12:
Guardian Angels

Regardless of your religious background, it is likely that you have heard of Guardian Angels and have seen the many different interpretations that people have of these entities. But, what are they exactly? What sets them apart from spirit guides and are there any real differences between the two?

Well, defined simply, Guardian Angels are entities which are assigned to a particular person, a group of people, a country or even a kingdom. Evidence of people's belief in them can be found throughout all of antiquity. However, the concept that we're most familiar with today, that which recognizes the hierarchy within the host of angels, was developed in Christianity. This is also one of the reasons why Guardian Angels—or just angels in general—are typically associated with this religion.

They work in the same manner as spirit guides. They can provide people with insight and help them along the path of spiritual development. At the same time, they are also capable of protecting their ward from any negative influences. In fact, there are cases of guardian angels performing "miracles" and saving people from grave danger. From helping them avoid accidents to healing the sick and dying, Guardian Angels are basically the whole package.

That being said, their function goes beyond guiding and protecting. Unlike your spirit guides, it has been said that these angels are also record keepers. Yes, they follow your every thought, everything you say and do, and then pass this information on to higher-ranking angels. What happens to the records? They get added to the universe's official records and basically detail your entire lifetime of good, and bad deeds. In certain religious beliefs, this is what they would use during your day of judgment. It is through these records that it is decided whether you're going to enter the pearly gates of heaven or be sent to an eternity of punishment, languishing in hell. *A scary notion, isn't it?*

Communicating with your guardian angel is possible too. Most people would speak to them in the same way they do with friends. You can ask them for counsel and comfort during troubled times or request for protection if you're going into a dangerous undertaking. There are prayers meant for Guardian Angels too, but do know that they are not worshipped in any way. Think of them as an invisible friend who never leaves your side; always listens and will be there for you no matter what you do in life. All you really need to do is call upon them.

So, are they the same as your spirit guides? Some people would agree, however, most others would not. The difference lies in their purpose and how they work. Whilst spirit guides work individually, the Guardian Angels follow a hierarchy and essentially work for a higher power.

Conclusion

Thank you again for downloading this book!

I hope this book was able to help you learn more about spirit guides!

The next step is to put this information to use, and begin using the strategies provided to communicate with your spirit guide.

Also don't forget to download my **FREE** report on the 7 Keys for Successful Meditation by following the link - http://bit.ly/1F91lfl

Finally, if you enjoyed this book, please take the time to share your thoughts and post a review on Amazon. It'd be greatly appreciated!

Thank you and good luck!

Printed in Great Britain
by Amazon